"Whether you're an aspiring, first-time, or veteran VP of Sales, Scott Leese's *More Than a Number* is more than a book. It's a guide, a reference manual, a peek into the brain and systems that have generated $100Ms in recurring revenue. But it's about more than the numbers—it's about how to do it the *right* way, for you and for your people. *More Than a Number* will help you elevate your team, your results, and your life."

—Kevin "KD" Dorsey,
VP Sales at PatientPop

"Becoming a VP of Sales is tough, and staying employed as one is even harder. Nobody is looking out for you except for you. What I love about this book is how Scott goes out of his way to help coach and mentor sales leaders so they have the best chance to succeed while doing things the right way. *More Than a Number* is everything Scott has learned over the course of a masterful career and should be required reading for anybody getting into sales leadership."

—Justin Welsh,
SaaS Sales Advisor

"A *must*-read for anyone in sales leadership or thinking about moving into sales leadership. Once again, Scott has an amazing vision to take what feels complex and theoretical, break it down to a human level, and give tactical advice."

—Richard Harris,
Founder at The Harris Consulting Group

"He's the truest advocate of being a VP Sales, and he's done it time and time again at the highest level. I wouldn't trust anyone else with this information besides Scott. So tune in, pay attention, take some notes, and execute on the advice he gives you."

—Morgan Ingram,
Director of Sales Execution and Evolution
at JB Sales Training

MORE THAN A NUMBER

The Modern VP Sales Playbook

Scott Leese

Scott Leese Consulting

More Than a Number: The Modern VP Sales Playbook

Scott Leese

Published by Scott Leese Consulting
Copyright © 2021 by Scott Leese
All rights reserved.

Scott Leese Consulting
PO Box 91462, Austin, TX 78709-0954
E-mail: scott@scottleeseconsulting.com

Limit of Liability/Disclaimer of Warranty:

Publishing and editorial team:
Author Bridge Media, www.AuthorBridgeMedia.com
Project Manager and Editorial Director: Helen Chang
Publishing Manager: Laurie Aranda
Cover Art Design: Ryan Parker

Library of Congress Control Number: 2020925705

ISBN: 978-0-9984054-9-0 -- paperback
978-0-9984054-8-3 -- ebook

Ordering Information:

Quantity sales. Special discounts are available on quantity purchases by corporations, associations, and others. For details, contact the publisher at the address above.

Printed in the United States of America

DEDICATION

This book is dedicated to all the sales leaders who were thrown into the middle of the ocean and survived. We've always been more than a number, and it's time we let 'em know. A very special shout out to the inspiration behind "Scotty's Little Sales Club." Guess I did OK after all.

CONTENTS

ACKNOWLEDGMENTS

I want to thank my family—Janet, Brayden, and Caleb—for helping me stay on task and forcing me to complete this project so we could go play; Richard Harris, my partner in Surf and Sales (surfandsales.com), for his friendship, guidance, and support; and Amy Volas, my partner in Thursday Night Sales (thursdaynightsales. com), for her motivation and inspiration; thank you to the Author Bridge Media team for your editorial and publishing assistance in creating this book. And finally, a big thank you to everyone who read and enjoyed *Addicted to the Process*: you convinced me that writing another book was a good idea.

Thanks to Ryan Parker for cover design input and assistance.

Special thanks to "heretic : the agency" for wordsmith/ design/editing assistance.

INTRODUCTION

The World of Sales

Sales is all about hitting numbers.

As a sales professional—whether a Sales Director, VP of Sales, or CEO/Founder—you know that hitting sales numbers is critical to your career and business growth.

But that growth brings new pressure.

Regardless of your title, expectations will run high, turnover is even higher, and the hours are long and brutal. You're accountable not just for your own success but for your team's success. Sure, you're making a healthy base salary with commissions and bonuses, but what you're really gunning for is that VP of Sales position. The prestige and compensation are greatest, and without that promotion, you can't buy that house, support your family, or see the world. Only one person will eventually be promoted. How do you make sure it's you?

Maybe you're a VP of Sales (or VP Sales, as we tend to call it). You've landed the coveted role, but you may be stretched near the breaking point. You'd never admit it, but deep inside, you have nights of anxiety, bouts of depression, and a sense of instability. You're making huge decisions that impact not just your life but all of the people below you. When sales goals aren't met, you're often the first one who's let go, and certainly, the first one to blame when sales numbers are down.

Sure, the new role brings prestige, respect, and more income. But you wish someone had told you about a manager texting you at ten o'clock at night expecting you to have a presentation ready by eight o'clock the next morning. About being given sales goals without the team to support it. About the tension with engineers who don't understand the need for certain features in order for you to sell the product and hit your goals. And if you make the decision to leave a toxic work environment, you can be blacklisted in the job market as a job hopper. Any new job you go to will want to know the track record you had at the job you just left, and they don't care about extenuating circumstances.

Maybe, as a CEO/Founder, you have so much at stake in your business. You may have mortgaged your home, your relationship, and your life to start and keep this business going. Sales success fuels its growth. Buy-in from shareholders and other investors, support from your board of directors, and the company's prestige in the marketplace are all on the line. Now you have to primarily rely on someone else to guarantee sales, without which your company will fail. You probably started the business out of your passion and expertise in a particular field, and that wasn't sales. Now you have to manage a VP of Sales and ensure he/she will produce, so you hit your business plan targets and make returns for your investors.

People often mistakenly view sales leadership roles as a path to getting rich and less often aim for the position for the right reasons. Successful candidates wind up stuck in a position they're not ready for, fighting tooth and nail just to keep their heads above water. CEOs and Founders have no idea how to support them and provide unreasonable expectations that don't get pushed back against. It's a vicious cycle that has led to VPs of Sales having an average tenure of less than eighteen months.

It doesn't have to be that way. Learn how businesses operate and fuel your desire to lead, coach, and inspire other salespeople. Let me show you what sales leadership can be and how it can change your life.

A Definition and Path Forward

Whether you're a Sales Director, a VP Sales, or a CEO/Founder, this book lights the path ahead, showing you how to reach your goals and enjoy the rewards.

If you're a Sales Director, I guide you in preparing for your dream VP Sales role: a higher base salary, larger bonuses and commissions, ownership of companies, and stock options. With those perks, it's no wonder the Vice President title is so appealing. I'll take you through exactly what it means to be a VP of Sales, what skills you need to succeed in the position, and what paths you can take to get there.

If you're a VP Sales, I show you how to manage expectations from your CEO, build a team that will excel, and drive your career forward. I want you to do more than just survive. I want you to *thrive*. That's why we start at the very beginning, walking through a comprehensive playbook that includes every aspect of how to succeed as a VP Sales.

If you're a Founder or CEO, the more you can understand the mindset and mentality of salespeople and what they go through, the better it will make you as a leader. I give you insight into what motivates your sales leader and how to set goals for them that are both realistic and aspirational. Find out how to keep them in the position in a way that works—both for them and for you.

From Zero to $25 Million

I know exactly where you're at and how to get where you want to go. I've ground it out as a Sales Director, VP Sales, and even CEO and Founder. At one company, I started the sales division, taking them from zero to $25 million annual recurring revenue (ARR) in roughly two years. As a VP Sales at Qualia, I went from zero paying customers to capturing almost 20 percent market share in just three years. Now, as the CEO and Founder of my sales consulting firm, Scott Leese Consulting, and Surf and Sales, I've assisted CEOs/VPs of Sales and other revenue leaders with sales strategy, process, pitch, and more.

My passion has grown from working inside one sales organization to helping others direct and improve their own sales organizations and careers. I want to uplift the profession of sales and grow businesses in healthy ways. Most importantly, I want to help you change your life.

A Playbook for Many Paths

In your role, you might feel like you are just a number in the company. But you are more than your sales targets; your results are more than that. When you learn this playbook, your life becomes *more than a number.*

Use the strategies I share with you to upend the status quo. If you are a sales director, walk the path for your promotion to VP Sales. Gain a greater sense of confidence and clarity, and learn how to motivate your team. If you are VP Sales, take these lessons and transform your position into one that gives you not only prestige but also respect. Work better with other executives, define your playbook, and get serious about work/life balance. If you're a CEO/Founder, use these tactics to build a stronger relationship with your VP Sales. Focus on sales growth and working together for the good of the company by understanding who your VP Sales is and where they're coming from.

You'll come away with the information you need to make positive change, building a better career and a better future for yourself and your company. By following these steps, you will improve your life, establish or protect your legacy, and have either a healthier career as a VP, or a stronger relationship with your VP.

Before you know it, you'll go from wherever you are now to wherever you want to be.

Chapter 1

Road Map

Action Is Success

Sales success comes from shrinking the delta between idea and action. The faster you can make something happen, the faster success will arrive.

At each level the delta changes. In my experience, when you understand the delta for each stage, the faster you will be able to maximize results for the level you are at, then grow to the next level.

I've Seen the Business from Every Side

As you know, I've had success in the three key roles of sales: Director, VP Sales, and CEO/Founder. I made my own path and I didn't have a guide. But my mistakes and successes along the way became a playbook for my success at each level. I tripped on a lot of bricks, and I hope you don't have to do the same.

I first got into sales to support my family. A long-running illness in my twenties left me with no formal training, and diving into sales was the best way for me to make up for lost time. Starting as a novice salesperson, I went in blindly but with a determination to be successful, and I quickly became the number one salesperson at my company. When it was time to move up, I applied to be a sales manager.

After being passed over in favor of someone with more tenure and despite the disappointment, I doubled down and broke my personal sales record while sharing with my teammates what was working for me. Three months later, the role became available again, and I put my name forward. This time, I landed the sales manager job and quickly learned the skills and strategies needed to grow into an effective Sales Director.

When I was ready to move from Sales Director to VP of Sales, I once again faced a challenge. I sat down with the current VP Sales and the CEO and asked, "How can I continue to advance here? What's the track to become a VP Sales?" They point-blank told me, "You'll never be a VP here. You don't have enough experience." So, I left.

In order to grow, I immediately landed a job as a VP Sales at another company. At the old job, my former boss sneered, "Scotty's little sales club will never succeed." I was deeply insulted, but nothing was going to motivate me more to succeed in my new role than proving people wrong.

In that first role as VP Sales, I grew the start-up rapidly in three years. Then I reached yet another ceiling and moved to another company. In my second stint as a VP Sales, I experienced real failure for the first time. My team didn't make a single sale in eight months (well, technically, we did, but the Founder and CTO killed the deal.) The product wasn't ready to be shipped, there was no alignment on how we would onboard new hires, and leadership did not tell us what we could actually sell. These experiences not only taught me the true pressures of a VP Sales role, but they allowed me to develop strategies needed to grow and succeed as well. Trainers can tell you how to do it, but you won't know until you get in and fail a few times. That adversity from experience will only help you succeed.

After about seven years embedded in various sales leadership positions, I finally understood the pressure that Founders face from investors, the Board, and other competitors or stakeholders. That pressure cascades from the Board to the Founder and down to the VP Sales. My own business has not needed investment capital, but it has given me the perspective needed to coach Founders and CEOs in leading their sales teams.

After spending twenty-some-odd years in sales, I have truly seen the business from nearly every angle. My first book, *Addicted to the Process: How to Close Transactional Sales with Confidence and Consistency*, gives you foundational knowledge on how to make sales. I show sales professionals how to sell consistently in a system that I call the Addiction Model of selling (pain, value, urgency, solution). The book became an Amazon #1 bestseller and a sales training standard. It also helped me land industry awards as a sales leader.

This book, *More Than A Number: The Modern VP Sales Playbook,* takes you to the next level as a sales professional, focusing on growing true sales leadership. It takes you into the trenches of each role, so you know what to expect and how to crush it. From Sales Director to VP of Sales to Founder/CEO, I want to give you the lowdown that no one else has the guts to tell you and the playbook for each role.

The Path Toward Sales Leadership

As a sales leader, you're ready for the next delta to quickly turn your ideas into action. This modern sales playbook shortens that delta as you grow in each role.

This book is divided into three sections, focusing on each of the three roles: Sales Director, VP Sales, and CEO/Founder.

Section 1: The Path to VP of Sales: *How to Land a VP of Sales Role*

For anybody who wants to get a promotion, this road map clearly defines the steps and skills you need to master.

- Investigate the VP Sales role. What is it, and are you sure you want it?

- Know your goals. How are you being measured, and what is a good opportunity?

- Be a great sales director through tactics and processes.

- Leave a great legacy. Turn entry-level reps into great salespeople.

Section 2: The VP of Sales: *How to Survive and Thrive as a VP of Sales*

This playbook empowers you to be a VP of Sales in a healthy way that still creates positive outcomes for your company. Reclaim your time—and your power.

- Define your own process and implement it.

- Create a solid sales culture, take responsibility, and empower people with the right tools.

- Build a strategy for long-term success, including: pricing structure, ideal customer profile, customer relationship management (CRMs), and other concrete solutions.

- Know how to manage and set expectations with other executives.

Section 3: The CEO/Founder–VP of Sales Dynamic: *How CEOs and Founders Can Empower and Support a VP of Sales*

Learn not only how sales leaders think, but what they want and need in order to be successful.

- Set goals for your VP Sales that are direct and anchored.

- Support, motivate, and develop your VP Sales.

- Increase their tenure and keep them long-term.

Regardless of which role you're in now, I recommend you read the entire book. You'll find important insights into how others view you, the challenges ahead, and where to go next. Then you can go back and reread the sections most relevant to you. As you grow into the next position, you'll know how to lead others, as well as interact with those in other roles.

The journey may be challenging as a sales leader, but as your possibilities expand financially, professionally and personally, you'll come to find it's well worth the rewards.

Let's start with the role of Sales Director.

Lack of boundaries: Your time is a little less your own the higher you go. You're expected to be available 24/7. Sure, they'll tell you this isn't true, but setting healthy boundaries can mean risking your reputation. Know what you're signing up for.

High alert: You're on edge all the time. There's a lot of anxiety, and you have to learn to deal with it in a healthy way. Congrats on hitting Q3's sales target; tomorrow is day one of Q4, and you're at 0 percent to goal again. Cue stress.

Length of stay: Eighteen months. That's the average tenure of a VP Sales today. You'll have, on average, six months to put processes and people in place. Then your bosses expect to see tangible results. But a sales cycle can be as much as twelve months, so what can you do? I personally know people who've had one full sales cycle, didn't produce, and were fired. And even though it's common, being labeled as a job hopper can hurt your future career. That means you want to be very sure that you can succeed before you make the leap.

Clear Expectations

To reach your goal, the next thing you need to know is how to move up. Ask your bosses what concrete success looks like and get that defined clearly and specifically.

In most companies, sales managers are in charge of sales reps, sales directors are in charge of sales managers, and VP Sales is in charge of the sales directors. But you don't always have to be a sales director to move up to VP.

Maybe your managers expect you to eclipse a million dollars in sales or work as a sales manager for three years. Maybe they expect you to be a stellar sales director for half a decade before you move up. Whatever those milestones look like in your company, you need to get them defined. Then you can set about finding ways to hit those targets.

Build up your career within a strong sales team. Have demonstrable leadership skills, great coaching, and successful sales cycles. You should be in the top 5–10 percent of your sales team to get in the running for sales manager, and sustain that ranking over time. To be in the running for a VP Sales role, you better be the best of all the sales managers or sales directors.

Know Your Strengths

Your next sales job can make or break your career. It's critical to find one that suits your skills and interests. When I first got into sales, I got a job in a transactional sales environment because I knew that I had very low patience and that I love to win. I had the chance to go home feeling like a winner every single day and that velocity behind the sales cycle suited me.

Soon after that, I had an opportunity to move to a huge oil and gas company. They had a really long, complicated sales cycle, but it was going to pay significantly more. I was flattered and excited about the prospect of it, but as soon as I told my wife about it, she laughed out loud. "You can't do that job! You don't have the patience for it." I knew right away that she was spot on.

One of the best things you can do is know yourself. Be self-aware about your strengths and weaknesses; put yourself in an arena that gives you the best opportunity to succeed.

Find a Safe Outlet

As you pursue your goal, make sure to find creative outlets to deal with the pressure and stress of the job. That could be exercise, meditation, or proper use of vacation and digital detoxing.

It's not sustainable for you to just go to happy hour, knock down two double Jack and Cokes, come home, have two more, and go to bed. By the time you're my age, you might have a bad liver and a lot of regrets. It's imperative to find healthy ways to deal with stress today.

Find mentors and peers to talk to—supportive people who know what you're going through. You aren't alone.

If you've read this chapter, and you're sure that you're ready to embark on this journey to VP Sales, the next step is to make sure you're more than just a good sales manager or sales director. Because it's great sales managers who become VPs.

Chapter 3

Greatness

How to Become Great

A VP of Sales is only as good as their weakest team member.

During one of my tenures as a VP Sales, I hired a new salesperson who was just out of prison. A lot of doors were closed on him, but I saw something in him. I knew I could develop him into someone who would be more than just good at his job; he could be great.

I coached him on how to be an inside sales professional and focused on his general life skills. With help, he became a strategist; always looking forward, giving himself concrete goals, and meeting them almost every time. Within a few years, he grew into a sales manager and eventually a VP Sales running a team of one hundred.

What I love about sales is it's a team sport. As a sales manager or sales director, your primary responsibility is to deliver results. That means delivering the numbers that people expect from you, but it also means developing a team that's capable of hitting those numbers. It's about attracting and retaining the right colleagues.

The sales manager's job is to empower the people they're managing to become as productive as possible. You need to help your team become better people, not just better salespeople. Invest in your people, and they will invest in your process and help catapult you to greatness. They will help you change your life and become the kind of VP you're proud of.

How do you become more than just a good sales manager? As you see in this chapter, you get serious about elevating your people and creating a team that's on the ball, every time. Then, you think about your own brand. Who are you outside of the office, and how is that helping you be the greatest version of yourself?

What Kind of Sales Manager Becomes VP Sales?

First, let's explore the stuff behind great sales managers.

Good sales managers will do what's asked of them, but that's it. *Great* sales managers do what's asked of them, and then they go further. They say, "Hey, we've talked to a couple of prospects who are outside of the target we're selling to, but there's been a really good response there. I think that we should go after that group."

It's those great sales managers who become VPs.

As you move further up the food chain, you're expected to have all of the same skills as a sales manager, and especially those you'll learn as a sales director. But you also need to show initiative and the ability to think strategically. You have to constantly iterate and improve, not just keep the ship pointed in the same direction. That means suggesting changes to the demo. It means pushing the product in a particular direction. It even means running recruiting events and building a personal brand for yourself online.

Justin Welsh, former VP of Sales at PatientPop, says that being successful as a VP of Sales is less about sales than you might think:

"Being a revenue executive means gaining consensus from your peer group and driving decisions or change in your organization." That means getting good at data interpretation, cross-functional compromise, and having tough conversations.

Here are a few other areas to focus on.

Deliver Results from Your People

As a VP, results are no longer just about your success. You should start getting comfortable with that process while you're still a sales manager or sales director.

Think of yourself as a developer of talent. Maybe you have a team member who's having a tough time sticking to goals that they set. Or maybe they have a weak sales pitch. Make them pitch over and over again while listening to their cadence and the tone of their delivery.

Don't be afraid to get really granular when you're chasing greatness. The ex-con I hired was incredibly well-spoken, but his writing skills weren't great. In the modern sales world, more and more communication is done over email, so it was hurting him. We worked on his grammar, his punctuation, even basic sentence structure. Soon he was performing well and had become a strong member of the team.

Diversify Your Income Potential and Brand

VP Sales positions are scarce, and thousands of hungry candidates determined to make the leap (just like you) are competing for them. You have to find ways to stand out from the pack, and that means diversifying your income and branding yourself.

This can mean specializing in any area you are passionate about, for example, real estate, stock investing, and content creation. Sales in these areas of expertise can help ease the economic pressure and worry if you don't hit quota.

Networking is also key. Build a group of people around you who share your pain, who've been through this, and who have found solutions. These are people who can—and will—help you if you ever find yourself in trouble.

If you're able to get on a podcast, that's great. It can bring in new business while simultaneously building credibility as a leader. That will help you feel secure in the job you're at and will also help you if, and when, you're in the job market the next time.

Create the DNA of Your Department

Your department defines your success. But not everybody is you. You can't just snap your fingers and insist they have the same level of confidence and skill that you do. Be patient. Create processes that live and breathe in your organization's DNA so that your team can easily come on board.

Continue to monitor your team. Make sure they're doing the activities you suggest every single day. That means that they're keeping all their data clean and accurate. It means that they're getting good at forecasting this month, as well as for the quarter, and even for the year. And it means they're good at following up with people and setting clear next steps.

You have to help your team bring the deals in, so there's also going to be contract negotiations. This could be over price, length of the agreement, or features that the prospect feels are mandatory but that you don't have yet. It's your job to do anything that you can to aid the team in their performance. Getting to that result is ultimately what matters. You'll find greatness together as a team, or you won't find it at all.

Once you've built a team that's consistently hitting its targets, you want to think about how that team will grow and excel without you. In the next chapter, I show you how to create a legacy for the future, something that will survive long after you've moved on or up.

Chapter 4

Legacy

How to Build a Legacy

You now know that your main mission as a sales leader is to develop talent. That's why your next step to becoming a VP Sales is to create a legacy that survives you. You want somebody who will succeed if they replace you one day when you move on. That means constant coaching to help your team maintain their greatness once you're no longer at the wheel.

Part of coaching your team is teaching them to have influence—not just on their direct reports, but also in the sales community as a whole. They should be working on creating a personal brand that elevates both themselves and your company. That can mean writing blog articles and posts, creating an email newsletter, or writing a book. They could be heavily contributing to communities like LinkedIn, being regular guests on podcasts, or speakers at events.

When you develop talent properly, you're creating a legacy for your company. When you change people's lives, they then become something more than they were, and they pass that down. They'll always remember the people who helped them along the way, and you'll be one of those people. There are few rewards greater than this and no better way to elevate your position and find the happiness you deserve.

Start with a focus on your people. Learn to trust and support them, and get your ego out of the picture. A legacy is all about what happens when you walk away from what you've built.

Turn Entry-Level Reps into Great Salespeople

To be a good VP of Sales, you have to love being a teacher. Start sharpening that skill at your current position. You won't have the time to learn how to teach once you're already a VP.

You've got to simplify complex products, decisions, and messaging with patience. You can't just tell somebody to do something one way, one time, and expect them to get it and do it perfectly. It will take dozens and dozens of times. Just think of how long it took you to become this good!

If somebody's asking you to spend some extra time and work with them, it's a sign of their dedication and determination. Let that get you fired up and inspired! You're nurturing people's careers and playing a huge part in their lives, which is what led you to this role in the first place: that feeling. Somebody gave you a chance once; this is your opportunity to pay it forward.

Delegation Is Key

You've hired solid people around you and under you. Great. Now you've got to trust them and get out of their way. You can't exist as a superhero. Leaving a legacy means learning how to delegate.

This is something that a lot of executives have a really hard time with. One of the things that I find helpful is to change your expectations of delegation. A task doesn't have to come back to you completed 100 percent to your satisfaction in order for it to be worth sending out. If they've gotten you halfway there, it has still saved you a lot of time. Plus, it gives you an opportunity to coach them, so they'll be even closer to the mark next time.

Then, when they do well, you're communicating back to them that you're proud of them. Validation is a key element in this environment.

The degree that you entrust your people to get things done not only gives you time to decompress but also helps build trust. You're giving them opportunities to do things that they haven't had a chance to do before, and that's really motivating. Empowering your team is never something you will regret.

Kick Out Your Ego

To do everything I've described here, it's incredibly important to get your ego out of the way. You can't go into sales leadership if you're looking for all the glory and all the credit.

That's one of the reasons why the number-one salesperson very rarely makes a great VP. In order to be the best salesperson out there, you've got to be a bit self-centered. That myopic focus is what makes you so great at what you do, but it becomes really hard to transfer that focus when your performance is no longer measured by just you.

When you start building your legacy, and you want to train someone to replace you when you move up to VP Sales, look for someone with a history of being a *good* salesperson who's great periodically. More importantly, look for someone who's more interested and fulfilled by helping other people get better.

Then, help them get better—not just at what they do, but at what they want to do next. Kevin Dorsey, current VP of Sales at PatientPop, learned that through his own career:

"Every promotion I have gotten in my sales career has been overwhelmingly anticlimactic, because I had already been doing the role long before the title was actually mine, and that is the piece that so many people miss the mark on when they are seeking a promotion. You need to start developing the skill necessary to do the next job *before* you have that job."

Identifying the people around you who are ready to be coached is an important part of the VP sales' playbook. But the road map doesn't stop there; you need consistent results in a variety of areas. Next, let's look at how a VP Sales achieves that by following a simple playbook.

Chapter 5

VP of Sales Playbook: How to Survive and Thrive as a VP of Sales

How to Create Your Own Sales Process

If you want to be the best you need a clear sales process. Creating those processes can be a challenge, but it can be done if executed well.

At one company that I consulted with, the Founder and their brand new head of sales asked what their sales priorities should be. I told them that in order to be great, you have to know exactly how to operate: what items to focus on, what order to do them in, and how to do them. I put together a framework for them to follow which came to be known as: a VP Sales playbook.

You're either a new VP Sales, or you're accelerating in this position. Maybe you're at a new company trying to build something that's your own. Either way, you need a clear blueprint for action. In these next chapters, I'll unveil the playbook, culture, strategy, and relationship-building mastery you need to excel.

In order to lead your sales teams and collaborate with other company leaders with strength and ease, the playbook is where it starts. As shared in this chapter, the playbook lays out how to interact with clients and customers, how to build and define your sales processes, and what sales materials you need. It's all about execution—and how you get it done.

A Strategy for Brilliance

Here are the key elements of the VP Sales playbook:

Become an industry and product expert. Don't be afraid to ask questions or show ignorance. There will always be a learning curve when entering a new company or position. Novice to expert. Embrace that!

- Learn the industry. What are the key terms in the industry? Who are you selling to? What are the pains in the industry?

- Learn the workflow for your team. What are the steps they're completing in order to get the job done? How long does it take?

- Learn the product. What are the features? What pain does it solve? How is it used?

Your job is only going to become more complex as you take on more responsibility. Do the learning you need to do now, at the beginning, while you have the time and energy.

Fight the urge to make a really big contribution. It isn't about making a huge splash right out of the gate! I've seen a lot of people fail by wanting to immediately start closing big deals. But without a solid foundation, it's doomed to fail. Y.O.R.O—You Only Ramp Once—so take advantage of the time in the beginning to learn all you can.

Build a sales process. It's up to you to consider the existing sales tools in your tech stack and see if they're the best ones. Don't just take over what your predecessor had in place. (Unless you love it.)

What will your sequences look like? What tone will you use to communicate? How many touches

will you put on the account every twenty-one days or
every six months? If you call someone and they don't
pick up, how long do you wait until you call them
again?

- Keep your CRM data up to date at all times.
  The data should be cleaned and scrubbed and
  accurate in real time.

- Iron out the contract and payment process.
  How exactly are you closing deals? How do
  clients pay? Is there an invoice?

Build your sales materials. Once you build these doc-
uments, make sure to share them with your team.

- **Objection rebuttal document**: This comple-
  ment to a sales script is a list of rebuttals to
  common objections. You should have a slightly
  different version of it for cold calls, product
  demos, and emails. For email communication,
  make different scripts ready for every scenario:
  prospecting emails, follow-up emails, "Missed
  you at today's demo; can we reschedule?" emails,
  and closing emails.

- **A return on investment (ROI) calculator**: Build an ROI calculator to show exactly how much prospects stand to save and gain with your product or service.

- **A competitive landscape document**: Show your sellers how your product stacks up against the competition. Include the ways in which the competition is inferior to your product. However, don't forget to acknowledge the ways in which they're superior and why their prospects should still go with you. Include cost comparisons, integrations, and anything else that sets you apart.

Use free trials sparingly and intelligently. It's important to think about how to convert free trials into paying customers. If you don't have that strategy in place, all you're doing is giving your product away for free.

Focus on the Execution

The playbook gives you the groundwork to get started in your new position, but it's important to remember to focus on execution. That means knowing, setting, and hitting your recruiting, revenue, and pipeline goals.

It also means defining your sales philosophy. In *Addicted to the Process*, I wrote about the addiction model for sales. You find the pain, build value, create urgency, and discuss the solution. That's my sales philosophy—but there are many others. Do some research, and see where you best fit. Remember that customer-centric models are more important than ever.

Finally, know how to package the product. Are you bundling everything together, or is it being sold à la carte? How many pricing options are you giving? Is it on a user license, or usage basis, or a flat fee? Some of that may already be decided if you're not coming on board with a new product. Still, make sure to examine why those decisions were made and if they're still the best for the sales process.

Once you start sitting down to actually make the calls and send the emails, you have to start tracking your key performance indicators and metrics. Are the tactics you're deploying effective? Getting a good sense of that data will help you execute in the end.

As a VP Sales, it starts by building a business you're proud of; a place where you'd want to work. That means you stay positive and hire a diverse team. Treat people respectfully, focus on results, make sure your team has all the right tools, and create a culture that prioritizes personal and professional growth.

If you can build a culture that works for you and your team, you'll be able to move forward with confidence and clarity. You'll become a better boss by creating a better experience than many sellers have ever had before. And by changing the lives of your team, you'll change your own life too.

Build the Business You Want to Work In

Your culture starts with the literal environment where you work. Office environments and internal culture vary widely between departments. Even in our new remote working world, the cultural differences in departments and roles are very real. Engineers want to work in peace and quiet. Salespeople often don't want that.

Salespeople need to create energy. That energy creates emotion, and that emotion drives you to keep going and succeed after ninety-nine no's in a row. I don't want to be the only person in the office talking on the phone. I don't want to feel like there are twenty annoyed people sitting around just listening to me talk.

Not too long ago, I helped hire a new head of legal. One of the first things she said to me after sitting down in the office was, "How the hell do you guys get anything done in here? There's music playing. There are no offices. There are fifty people on the phone."

"Oh, wow," I said. "We might not be the right culture fit if this is your forever desk."

But she had a good point. "I have to review contracts all day long, and think clearly and focus," she said. "You're not going to be able to find any legal head who can get their job done, and done well, in this environment."

I knew my sales team wouldn't perform in silence, but she was right; the sales floor wasn't the right place for her. We moved her desk, and everyone was happier.

So how do you make sure that you're creating the kind of culture you want?

Stay Positive

The people we talk to have a million different plates they're spinning. It might not be the right time for them, or they might love everything but not want to a head of sales enablement or operations. The best use of my time as a head of sales isn't building reports in Salesforce. That's just one of the things sales ops is for.

I go into a new business knowing exactly what I need and what tools will help my team. So I want my sales ops team to be supportive and help me get things done. It's a great way to delegate and off-load some work on people who are really good at things that might not be your particular strength.

Creating a solid sales strategy is invaluable, but executing on it means getting your executives on board. That's why the next step to success as a VP Sales is working on your relationship-building skills with other department leaders.

Chapter 8

Relationships

Nobody's Superhero

When I first became a VP of Sales, I was beholden to a demanding CEO.

I was running myself ragged, trying to please my boss. But the more I exceeded his expectations, the more the expectations grew. I started getting messages at eight and nine o'clock at night, with tasks that were due sooner and sooner.

Eventually, I realized I was so determined to prove myself that I didn't establish any boundaries or communicate my needs. He wasn't a tyrant—I was a pushover.

It's an easy mistake to make, especially when you're trying to prove yourself early in your career. But over time, you'll learn to better utilize resources around you and understand that you can't do it all. That starts with setting boundaries and building better communication with your team.

Make sure you're clear with your team about how you like to be managed, treated, and communicated to. You certainly don't want to end up in an unpleasant or abusive working relationship like I did. Set hard times that you plan to sign off, and don't respond to emails or texts during off-hours or on weekends if you don't want to.

Once you've established clear boundaries, you need to work on communication with your team. That means building and maintaining strong, positive relationships, especially with those who are equal and above you in the hierarchy. Know what should reasonably be expected of you and what you can expect from others. You will also need to work on the relationship with your CEO, VP of Finance, VP of Marketing, VP of Customer Success, VP of Product or Engineering, and Human Resources (HR).

That's how you excel as a VP of Sales and how you make sure that you're having fun and becoming the best version of yourself. And when you do, you not only change your life, but the lives of everyone around you.

Relationship with CEO

The CEO is the most important relationship for you to develop because you're likely reporting to them. It is also likely going to be the most difficult relationship you have.

One of the most important things to do right from the start is to get clarity on goals and expectations. What do they expect from you, and what do you plan to deliver? Talk through hiring goals and revenue targets, and update them on progress and pacing. Collaborate and forecast the next twelve to twenty-four months of the business in terms of sales and growth. It's the CEO's job to push you in order to drive growth and drive revenue for the company. You're always going to be doing this delicate dance between what's possible and healthy, and what the CEO wants you to achieve. It's up to you to find a way to balance that push and temper it with realistic expectations.

Relationship with VP of Finance

One interaction that's likely new for a VP Sales is the VP of Finance: your gatekeeper who controls many of the things you need. This is the person who approves customer feedback, which the VP Product uses to improve the product, creating a tight loop between the customer and the product, says Joel.

Relationship with HR

As VP Sales, your people are your greatest resource. A huge part of your work is making sure you and your team are trained appropriately and that everyone on your team is happy, healthy, and safe. The head of HR is your partner in this area.

Talk to HR about what kind of roles you're looking for, and make sure they know the velocity that you need to scale your sales team. Some areas to get clarity on include the following:

- How can we source candidates and onboard effectively and quickly?

- What does the compensation need to be for these roles?

- What does the applicant pipeline look like?

- What's the target hiring date(s)?

- What do onboarding and training look like?

- How will the training be delivered?

Madison Butler, who has spent her entire career in human resources, says VP Sales and HR people are, in fact, working towards the same goal of creating thriving teams:

"Building relationships between teams is critical for the success of all teams, but more specifically sales," she says. "Relationships between sales and HR must be rooted in trust and the understanding that success is everyone's goal. Sales organizations need an environment where they can thrive, shine, and produce, and HR will be the key to helping curate that culture."

You Are Not an Island

You're in a very demanding role, potentially the most important role in the whole company. The majority, if not all, of the blame for failing to achieve revenue targets is going to fall on you. But you can't do everything yourself.

Learn to leverage the relationships around you. Make sure all your data is accurate so everyone is empowered to make the right choices. There's no way one person can do everything, but you aren't one person. You're a team.

Once you've built solid relationships with your

Chapter 10

Motivate

Leading Leaders

As a Founder or CEO, you've demonstrated your leadership. You've built an entire company and guided it to success. You're familiar with how to inspire your team.

But leading a VP of Sales is different because they're also a leader with a very particular relationship to their own team and to you. Understanding the motivations of your VP of Sales will help you be the best possible leader for them.

At one job where I was the SVP of Sales, the Founders admitted needing me because they didn't know what they were doing with sales. It was really empowering and motivating, but I also had a lot to learn from them in other areas. They brought me in on Board meetings, got me working in tandem with the product team, and supported my growth as I took on a guiding role on their entrepreneurial journey.

We had really powerful, open dialogue and mutual trust. I was able to align with the Founders on a winning strategy for launching a new organization. We leaned on the quality of the product and kept our prices low. Best product. Best prices. Best in class. That company is worth more than any other I've worked for.

That relationship worked so well because they knew I was motivated by inclusion and new opportunities. And if they kept me motivated, the entire company would do better. We created a strong, symbiotic relationship. You can do the same with your VP.

If you're a CEO, your first step is to support your VP Sales. Give them insight into what happens behind the scenes and space to do what they do best. Improve deals by removing barriers but keep them accountable. Above all, make sure they have a reason to stay.

Doing these things will ensure you build a stronger, more successful sales organization, which leads to helping build a better, more successful company and a better life for yourself. Create a better relationship with your VP, founded on mutual respect and understanding.

Peek behind the Curtain

One of the things that motivates the VP Sales is to give them access to everything going on behind the scenes. Allow your VP to attend Board meetings. It gives them important exposure and insight into how the Board thinks, how they communicate, and why the targets they need to hit matter so much.

The fundraising process is another area your VP probably isn't familiar with. It's not something that you learn about very often when you're an account executive or a sales manager.

I would also love to see Founders and CEOs recognize that a VP Sales is entrepreneurial. It's often said that one of the cool things about being in sales is that, in many ways, you run your own business. If someone has made it all the way to the VP Sales, the odds are that learning more about the entrepreneur's journey will be both motivational and impactful.

Money Makes the World Go Round

A VP Sales is, obviously, money motivated. I wouldn't say we're coin-operated, but we do like coins. If you're a Founder, you've got to recognize that this individual—with this mindset—is in charge of the machine that's bringing revenue into your company. Failure to do so, and failing to compensate appropriately, is going to cause problems.

Pay your VP Sales "market rate" or higher. That means you're giving them a motivational variable component to their compensation, which is often double the base salary. It should also include a significant equity stake (1%-3%) in the business. That's part of the allure and motivation, and it gives you an employee who has a real stake in making the company successful long term. At some point, these gigs all start to pay the same, and equity becomes increasingly important as VPs of Sales look to maximize their returns. Don't be a cheapskate here.

You want the VP of Sales to be motivated—not just to hit their number, but to build the entire business. That will keep them fighting tooth and nail to keep the business healthy. It will also keep them around longer, giving your sales org stability and continued leadership, which is good for everybody.

No One Likes Micromanagement

When leading a leader, you have to give them space to do what they're good at. I once ran a sales organization for a company with offices in four different cities across the country, in three different time zones. On one particular day, I got on a plane at seven o'clock in the morning and took a three-hour flight, then a cab ride to the office. When I got settled in, I found a set of increasingly desperate text messages, emails, and a voicemail from the Founder.

"Hey, what are our sales going to look like today?"

"Hey, you haven't responded. Everything looking good?"

"I know you're on a plane, but sales aren't very good today. What's your plan to turn it around?"

I was furious. I had traveled for hours. I hadn't even had a chance to eat lunch, let alone see how my team was doing. And we were talking about numbers for *half a day*.

It's so important to give your VP Sales the autonomy to do their job. One of the things that motivated them to get to this place is to have some level of autonomy and decision-making power. You hired this particular

VP for a reason. You've got to find a way to trust your people, get out of their way, and let them lead.

Focus on the tasks that you do best, and let the VP Sales do their thing.

How to Make Your VP Sales Accountable

Many CEOs are too hands-on because they want to make sure the VP of Sales is accountable. What they fail to realize is that nobody's neck is on the guillotine more than the VP of Sales.

I don't need to be reminded that if I don't hit my numbers, I'm going to lose my job. I know I am accountable. It's why I get paid what I get paid, and I know what I signed up for. Part of the reason I signed up for it is because I like that kind of pressure, and on some level, I like being the hero. But I don't need to be reminded of what's at stake three to four times a week. We get it!

All the data is there. There's total transparency, and it's there for you to take advantage of. Keep informed, but try to stay as hands-off as possible. Guide, support, enable, uplift, inspire. I can assure you that doubling down on "accountability" isn't what your VP Sales needs.

Improve Deals by Removing Barriers

As VP Sales, part of my job is to ask my sales team what's blocking them. My job is to remove those obstacles. What I can't remove, I take up the chain to the CEO or Founder.

If you're looking to motivate a sales leader, take the information they give you, and remove blockers and obstacles in the way of the selling process. If you are reading this and you're a VP Sales, I want you to ask yourself this question: When was the last time your CEO went to bat for you and quickly removed something blocking deals and projects? I fear too many of you just muttered "*never*" to yourselves.

Of course, there's a difference between an excuse and a real impediment to closing deals. It's up to you, as the Founder or CEO, to understand the difference and to be able to have that dialogue with the VP Sales. That will help you build a solid relationship that can endure some down months or quarters. As we see in the next chapter, building a strong relationship will allow you to retain that VP Sales for the long-term growth of the company.

Chapter 11

Retention

Turnover Is Expensive

The average tenure of a VP of Sales is eighteen months. That's it. That's a problem for VPs of Sales and CEOs alike because you're constantly starting from scratch rather than building on strengths.

You make a new hire. They get trained up, get a process in place, and get their people in place. That might take three months. Then they start building the pipeline. Their first deal isn't supposed to close for twelve months, but you're expecting to see results right away. The pressure compounds. If some of those deals don't close, Founders will often say, "You've been here for a little over a year now, and the numbers aren't there. We've got to let you go."

This happens all the time, and it's a huge mistake.

Every time there's a shift in management, your whole team is bogged down. Too much executive turnover is a signal that something's not right.

If you have a longer tenure for your VP Sales, you have more stability, and you increase the odds that the staff underneath them will stick around. You get consistent training, consistent messaging, and consistent delivery. You get a VP Sales who's as invested in the company as you are, and that changes your entire relationship. It changes your trajectory, your day-to-day work, and your life.

So how do you ensure that a VP's tenure is going to be long enough to make the odds of your company's success high? You provide them with external support, tools, and incentives beyond base pay, and you get better at giving positive feedback. You also need to stop dropping VPs every time the company does well by thinking you can top them off with somebody better who has done it before. Empowering your VP Sales to grow to the next level with the company allows you to capitalize on that industry knowledge and strength.

External Resources

One of the things that almost never happens is for new VPs of Sales to get coaching from somebody who's been there. Consider hiring a private coach or advisor who's been in the role before. They can guide the new VP Sales and provide valuable insight about their successes and failures.

If more Founders took that kind of approach, it would go a long way to helping the VP Sales succeed. And it isn't an expensive proposition. A good coach will save you more in the long run than whatever it costs you upfront.

Working Environment

VPs of Sales need positive reinforcement just as much as everybody else. But it's tricky because their results and failures are more visible than anybody else's. We take a lot of critique and criticism, as well the lion's share of the blame, when revenue numbers aren't achieved.

CEOs and Founders can do a better job bringing positive feedback to the VP Sales. Find ways to recognize them for their achievements. Mutual respect and appreciation for a job well done will help them get through the challenging times.

Tools

Many tools are available that make sales quicker, easier, and more trackable. That's key to long-term strategizing and success. If your VP is working with a team of three or four, they don't need much tech assistance. But a year later, when they're leading a team of a hundred, they are going to want tools that make their lives easier and the activities of their sales reps and managers visible.

If you want to support your VP Sales and keep them around, give them the budget to buy tools that will help them and their team perform and produce, with an eye on future growth.

Benefits Beyond Base Pay

I once had a milestone bonus that changed my trajectory with the company. I had been there for two years when we got to $10 million in ARR. For my bonus, I got a bump in stock options, which was a significant chunk.

I was extremely determined to hit that particular revenue milestone because I had something to look forward to. And at that point, I had to stay there for another year in order to vest. My next milestone was at $25 million, and since I had to be there for at least a year, I dedicated myself to try and hit that milestone.

And I did it.

If those milestones weren't in place and the motivation to stay for a year after hitting them, I would have considered leaving the organization much sooner than I did.

CEOs and Founders should be smart about the options and equity that they put in front of the people who are continuing to grow the business. VPs should also understand the minutiae of how this compensation works and what to ask for.

Experience Isn't Everything

Founders regularly put too much emphasis on experience. Often, a Founder will use a "green" VP Sales to get them from zero to $5 million. But when the company starts to take off, the CEO will decide that the VP doesn't have enough experience getting to the next stage. They say, "Troy has never taken a company from $5 million to $25 million before. But this guy Randy has. So, we're going to fire Troy and hire Randy."

And when Randy gets them to $25 million, suddenly

they're looking ahead again. "I don't know that Randy can get us to $100 million. He's never done it before."

So, they fire Randy and go out looking for someone who's gotten to $100 million before.

Amy Volas, the Founder and CEO of Avenue Talent Partners, saw this firsthand. She tells the story of a tech startup that "got caught up in the 'shiny objects' of a person's reputation."

At that company, the leadership "doled out a big CRO title and a seven-figure salary because the person came from 'their space,' and that's what they needed to do to land him," says Amy. "Fast forward sixteen months and $1.2M in hiring costs, and they were facing 50 percent customer churn and 65 percent team churn. The business was dangling by a thread."

"So, they fired him and hired a newer VP of Sales," Amy continued. "Two years later, the business had grown year over year, and their customer retention rates were at 89 percent."

There's clear evidence that you're not going to succeed just because you bring in somebody from the outside who's been there at a higher level. It's just not as simple as that.

Letting Go

Unfortunately, retention isn't always possible and it's necessary to let a VP Sales go. For example, when:

- the team underneath them is unhappy with their leadership,

- the culture has become negative or toxic,

- there's not enough coaching,

- they stop getting their work done, or they are tardy or delinquent on projects, or

- the results are not there, despite best efforts.

It's up to the VP and the Founder/CEO to work together to make retention possible. Only then can we break out of the negative patterns the industry is stuck in and improve success across the board.

Chapter 12

Delivery

Actions > Words = Momentum

You want to inspire your team. You want to grow from low, or even no, sales to a multimillion- or even billion-dollar business. Whether you're a sales manager, VP Sales, or CEO/Founder, the playbook for success is all about taking you from idea to action faster.

Shorten that delta as much as possible.

But sometimes, you overthink. Expectations are high, self-doubt overcomplicates every decision, leading you to become hyper-focused on the numbers. Use this playbook to overcome those doubts. Take hold of the opportunity, establish your goals, and find the motivation to succeed in whatever role you're in.

If you're a Sales Director considering the move up, you now know the good, bad, and ugly about the role. You know which skills you need to succeed in the position and the paths you can take to get there. You're ready to become a great VP Sales and leave a lasting legacy.

If you're already a VP Sales, you now have the playbook to be more effective and successful. Use this to grow in your current role and plan for your next role. Become the best practitioner in the field and go for your goals.

If you're a CEO, you now understand what motivates your VP Sales and how to build a strong culture of communication and collaboration. You're ready to move forward: armed with strong goal setting and VP retention, so your company will be at its strongest and ready to thrive.

Remember, you're *more than just a number.*

No matter where you are in your career, understanding this playbook will change your life. You will no longer be flying without a GPS. You'll feel uplifted. VPs of the future can, and should, have better situations than those of us who have walked the path already. And CEOs can have better relationships with their VPs.

With these strategies, be inspired to take the profession to the next level and make it better than when you started. That's my purpose for writing this book.

It's up to you to take the actions you need in order to build the life you want.

Walking the Talk

Sales has given me a life I never dreamed was possible. It gave me challenges, opportunities, and success; it provided me constant growth. And when I have an idea, I run with it. I love the thrill of building something new and helping others achieve their career goals.

Having been told I would never become a VP Sales, it was my determination that propelled me to take a chance. I left that job and set out to get what I wanted, taking action. Yet when I achieved everything I dreamed and became VP Sales, I faced a period where my team had no sales for eight months. I wondered if I would succeed in this position, but I learned valuable lessons about selecting the right company to work for and the right CEO to work for.

Eventually, I started my own company. As CEO and Founder of my own business, everything was on the line and wondered how successful I could be.

I've mastered the playbook for all three roles. And now you have the playbook too.

Looking back, I see that I have always been driven

by new challenges. That's why I founded a company that's always focused on the next horizon. I consult with top businesses, working with Founders or CEOs, VP Sales, and Sales Directors. Together we strategize and build their sales playbooks for multimillion-dollar sales machines.

I'm living *my* dream, helping companies build sales cultures. My hours are my own, I have healthy outlets for the pressure, and every day I'm helping other people break out of the negative cycle and make changes in their lives and careers.

I would love to see you grow in your journey, whatever step you're at. Connect with me through my website. Invite me for talks at your company. Or engage me with your team. You can also connect through the micro-community that I've built with sales alumni from Surf and Sales events. Or tune into The Surf and Sales podcast, which I run with my co-host Richard Harris. Join the "Thursday Night Sales" community, which I co-host with Amy Volas.

I'd love to hear your feedback on this playbook. Head over to Amazon and leave a review about your experience based on this book. Or, if you'd prefer a real conversation, you can engage with me on LinkedIn or Patreon. I'd love to see you there. You can join me and get messages and content that I produce, most of which I don't release anywhere else.

Whether you're looking for a connection, help, or advice from me, please reach out. Join some of the events that I do, or participate in some of the communities that I'm in. I'm here for you.

Now Is Your Time

I often tell people, "Sales can change your life." I mean it.

If you're reading this book, you're at a place in your life where you're considering a change. You're defining success for yourself. You're focused on leveling up, either for yourself or for your business. Sales, to me, continues to be a vehicle and a mechanism for us to do really good things in the world—to change our lives and the lives of others in a very impactful and meaningful way. Sales is an honorable and viable profession.

A lot of people have a negative view of sales. Hopefully, someday, we get to a place where our parents don't say things like, "You should have been a lawyer, Scott." I can proudly say, no, I should not have been a lawyer. I enjoy my life and my career. I've made sales into what I needed it to be: I'm able to give back and help people all the time.

That's the key to ongoing, permanent success. Make it more than just a job by understanding what success feels like to you, and then going out and getting it. Do something bigger and better. Your goal shouldn't just be to help yourself, but also to meaningfully help others along the way. That's what I'm talking about when I say that sales can change your life.

Your sales goal is never just a number. And nor is your life. With this playbook, you can achieve your dreams on your own terms and always be MORE THAN A NUMBER.

ABOUT THE AUTHOR

Scott Leese is a strategic advisor and Founder of Scott Leese Consulting, which focuses on helping companies scale from $0–$25M ARR. As CEO, Leese works with both domestic and international companies on sales strategy, process, people, pitch, and more.

Leese has a proven track record of lifting organizations to new heights with limited resources, but his passion has shifted to helping others direct and improve their own careers. He founded Surf and Sales in 2018 to provide an alternative to standard sales conferences. This microconference is now attended by top salespeople every year and continues to help people transform and grow their careers.

His first book, *Addicted to the Process*, is a #1 best seller focused on the addiction method of sales, helping individual contributors revitalize their careers.

Before founding his consultancy, Leese worked at every level of the sales hierarchy. As the Senior Vice President of Sales at Qualia, he went from zero paying customers or revenue to capturing 15 percent market share in just three years. As SVP Sales at OutboundEngine, he grew revenue by over 650 percent. The company was named to the Best Places to Work in Austin every year he worked there.

During his tenure as VP Sales at Main Street Hub, Leese built sales offices in Austin, San Francisco, New York City, and Los Angeles and was responsible for every aspect of the sales organization. He grew the team from 2 to 200, and Main Street Hub was acquired in 2018 by GoDaddy for $175 million.

Leese has spent his entire professional career building and scaling sales orgs at SaaS companies. Today he helps others follow in those footsteps.

WORK WITH ME

Contact information: scott@scottleeseconsulting.com
P.O. Box 91462
Austin, TX 78709
United States

Websites/Resources:
https://scottleeseconsulting.com
https://www.surfandsales.com
https://www.thursdaynightsales.com
https://www.patreon.com/thescottleese
https://scottleeseconsulting.com/get-the-book

Made in United States
North Haven, CT
02 July 2024

54318581R00059